Thailand Travel Guide:

Explore the Land of Smiles | Discover Culture, Cuisine, and Adventure

Lucian Whitlock

© **Copyright 2024 - All rights reserved.**

The contents of this book may not be reproduced, duplicated, or transmitted without the direct written permission of the author or publisher.

Under no circumstances will the publisher or author be held liable for any damages, recovery, or financial loss due to the information contained in this book. Neither directly nor indirectly.

Legal Notice:

This book is protected by copyright. This book is for personal use only. You may not modify, distribute, sell, use, quote, or paraphrase any part or content of this book without the permission of the author or publisher.

Disclaimer Notice:

Please note that the information contained in this document is for educational and entertainment purposes only. Every effort has been made to present accurate, current, reliable, and complete information. No warranties of any kind are stated or implied. The reader acknowledges that the author is not offering legal, financial, medical, or professional advice. The contents of this book have been taken from various sources. Please consult a licensed professional before attempting any of the techniques described in this book.

By reading this document, the reader agrees that under no circumstances will the author be liable for any direct or indirect loss arising from the use of the information contained in this document, including but not limited to - errors, omissions, or inaccuracies.

Table of Contents

Introduction 4

Chapter 1: Travel Essentials 11

Chapter 2: Must Visit Places In Thailand 19

    Bangkok: The Vibrant Capital 19

    Phuket: Tropical Paradise in the Andaman Sea 21

    Ayutthaya: Historical Marvels 22

    Krabi: Nature's Playground 23

    Sukhothai: Birthplace of Thai Civilization 24

    Pai: Tranquil Haven in the Mountains 25

Chapter 3: Itineraries 27

Chapter 4: Best Restaurants and Cuisine 31

    Bangkok's Street Food Extravaganza 31

    Exploring Northern Flavors in Chiang Mai 32

    Coastal Culinary Adventures in Krabi 33

    Phuket's Fusion of Flavors 34

    Thai Desserts and Sweet Endings 35

    Thai Street Drinks - Cool Refreshments for Every Palate 36

Chapter 5: Accommodations in Thailand 38

Chapter 6: Cultural Activities in Thailand 43

Chapter 7: Nightlife And Festivals In Thailand 48

Chapter 8: Souvenirs And Shopping In Thailand 53

Chapter 9: Photography and Social Media: 58

Chapter 10: Tips For Traveling in Thailand 62

Chapter 11: Frequent Asked Questions About Thailand 69

Conclusion 75

Introduction

Within the wide tapestry of locations all over the world, there is a world that contains the promise of unbounded joys and adventure. This world is woven into the fabric of the planet. Imagine a kaleidoscope of colors, the tantalizing scent of exotic spices, and the constant hum of a culture that is deeply rooted in tradition and filled with historical significance. What you are going to experience is going to be like this. Please accept our warmest greetings as we extend to you a warm welcome to Thailand, the breathtaking Land of Smiles. With each step that we made, a new chapter of an experience that was just waiting to be written was unveiled.

In the event that you have ever found yourself wishing you could escape the mundane routines of your everyday life and thinking about other places, what kinds of occurrences spring to mind? You may have silently wanted to immerse yourself in the vibrancy of a culture that has not been influenced by the passage of time, and you may have secretly wished to see photographs of ancient temples, bustling marketplaces, or beaches that are spotless. As a fellow nomad, I can assure you that you would not be the only one in that predicament. Thailand's fascination extends far beyond simple wanderlust, as it profoundly resonates with the spirit of each and every visitor. This is something that travelers who are looking for an experience that is unmatched will discover on their journey.

In spite of this, let's not sugarcoat the situation: turning a desire of travel into a reality frequently feels like traversing a convoluted maze. Making travel arrangements to a country outside of one's own can be an experience that is both tremendously exciting and worrisome at the same time. As if it were a never-ending checklist, the questions keep popping up, and they are as follows: Where should I go? And what should I look into for myself? What do I need to do in order to participate in the traditions of the region without accidentally upsetting anyone? You do not need to be concerned since you have discovered the resource that will enable you to uncover the mysteries that Thailand has to offer. The purpose of this travel guide is to serve as a reliable traveling companion for you as you embark on this journey through the distant lands of the planet.

Consider for a moment that you have the ability to make your trip fantasies come true. How would you feel? Imagine that all of the obstacles that are preventing you from taking in the wonders that Thailand has to offer could be removed, so allowing place for an experience that you will never forget. The contents of this book are more than simply a collection of pages; it is a guidebook that was written with your desire to travel in mind, and it is also your ticket to an experience that is completely immersive.

In light of this, let us now talk about the problem that is most obvious in the area (no pun intended). The process of travel planning may be both exhilarating and intimidating at the same time. It is possible that the joy may be overshadowed at times by the dread of making cultural mistakes, the fear of missing out on hidden treasures, and the confusion of where to begin things. Any one of these factors has the potential to bring about anxiety. You are experiencing the kind of annoyance that every tourist experiences, the kind that makes you wish you had a partner who is familiar with the complexities of the location that you have chosen to visit that you are currently experiencing.

It would be greatly appreciated if you would let our Thailand trip guide to serve as your personal travel advisor, providing answers to all of your concerns and assisting you in navigating the daunting number of options. This book is not simply a collection of data and figures; rather, it is a personalized experience that is designed to address your concerns, provide the answers to your inquiries, and most importantly, feed your passion for traveling.

When you read through these pages, you will find that there is more to learn than just the tourist attractions and useful advice that are presented here. This area is home to the pulsating heart of Thailand, filled with legends of long-gone civilizations, delectable cuisine, and magnificent landscape that varies from perfect beaches to deep jungles. Not only is this an offer to visit Thailand, but it is also an invitation to experience the pulse of the nation and to become a part of the narrative for Thailand.

For what reason have you entrusted this book with the responsibility of fulfilling your trip goals? Take into consideration that this is your very own backstage pass to the delights that Thailand has to offer, handpicked by someone who has experienced personally what it is that you are yearning for. Permit me to clarify this without appearing to be self-serving: the thoughts that are presented on these pages are those of someone who has a profound awareness of the nuances that are present in Thailand's vast cultural diversity. A person who has been to Thailand has had the opportunity to see the country's bustling marketplaces, its joyful celebrations, and its tranquil retreats.

Please read this book if you have ever been compelled to explore the unknown and if you have ever felt drawn to venture beyond the commonplace. This book is for you, dear reader. These pages provide the answers to the questions that will allow you to solve the riddles of the path that is waiting for you and will lead you to Thailand. To begin your journey around Thailand, are you prepared to turn the page and get started? When you finally make it to the Land of Smiles, we will be overjoyed. The journey is about to get underway.

The Science Behind Thailand

The Unique Blend of Tradition and Innovation

In addition to being a nation steeped in a colorful past and rich cultural heritage, Thailand is also a center for the growth of scientific research. This chapter looks into the fascinating topic of "The Science Behind Thailand," which investigates the ways in which this Southeast Asian nation has been able to successfully combine the most cutting-edge technology advancements with its traditional practices.

The Difference Between Traditional Medicine and Modern Medical Approaches

Without taking into account the traditional medical practices of the country, it is hard to have a conversation about the scientific advancements that have taken place in Thailand. Herbal medicines, massage therapy, and spiritual healing are all components of Thai traditional medicine, which has its origins in the spiritual healing practices of ancient Thailand. In spite of this, Thailand has recently made significant headway in the direction of modernizing its healthcare system by constructing hospitals and medical research facilities that are on the cutting edge of technology. As a result of the harmonious combination of modern and ancient medical practices, Thailand has emerged as one of the most popular locations in the world for travel for medical purposes.

2. The Importance of Innovation in Agriculture for Prospective Growth

Despite the fact that Thailand has a long history of agriculture, the country continues to make significant progress in agricultural research. Through the use of innovative farming methods such as hydroponics, organic farming, and precision agriculture, the country has established itself as a pioneer in the implementation of environmentally responsible agricultural practices. Researchers are utilizing technology to improve crop yields while also reducing the amount of damage done to the environment. The purpose of this action is to ensure that Thailand will continue to hold a prominent position in the global food production scene.

3. The protection of the natural world and animal and plant diversity

Because of the growing number of people throughout the world who are concerned about climate change, Thailand has emerged as a significant participant in the field of environmental conservation. Protecting the country's abundant biodiversity, which includes a wide variety of ecosystems ranging from verdant rainforests to incredible oceanic wonders, is a priority for the nation. For the purpose of preserving Thailand's natural wonders for future generations, scientific research activities are centered on gaining knowledge about endangered species and protecting them, as well as promoting practices that are sustainable.

4. Progress in Technology and in the Field of Space Travel

Thailand has shown that it is highly interested in space exploration and technology, despite the fact that it is unquestionably not a nation that is capable of space travel. The enhanced standing of Thailand in the international space community can be attributed to the country's investments in satellite technology as well as its collaborative efforts with other space organizations from other countries. There is a clear indication that the nation is dedicated to being at the forefront of technological progress, as seen by its decision to participate in activities relating to space.

5. Urban Planning and Communities That Are Smart

The bustling metropolis of Bangkok, which is located in Thailand, is a demonstration of the nation's dedication to putting smart city concepts into action all around the country. City dwellers in Thailand are becoming more ecologically sensitive and sophisticated as a direct result of the utilization of technology to improve urban living conditions. By harnessing the power of data and connections, the nation is working toward the goal of constructing contemporary cities that are environmentally responsible. As part of this, the development of advanced waste management systems and efficient public transit networks is under underway.

Biotechnology and pharmaceuticals come in sixth.

There is a possibility that the substantial expansion that the biotechnology and pharmaceutical industries have experienced in Thailand can be attributed to Thailand's dedication to research and development. It is possible for the nation to support efforts that aim to improve global health in addition to its own healthcare system because it is making significant progress in the manufacturing of pharmaceuticals, biotech products, and vaccines. The creation of partnerships between the public sector and the private sector is absolutely necessary in order to encourage innovation and ensure that Thailand will continue to maintain its prominent position in the international pharmaceutical arena.

The symphony of tradition and progress playing in perfect harmony

The intricate fabric of Thailand, which is woven with a beautiful combination of history and progress, is woven with the contributions of contemporary science. The scientific landscape of Thailand is as diverse as the cultural fabric of the nation. It encompasses everything from the most cutting-edge developments in biotechnology to the more time-honored healing practices of traditional medicine. It is because of Thailand's dedication to striking a balance between the preservation of its legacy and a forward-looking approach to science that the country will continue to be an unforgettable travel destination for individuals who are fascinated by the dynamic interplay of history and innovation.

Chapter 1:
Travel Essentials

Making the decision to travel to Thailand will unquestionably result in an experience that is both multifaceted and rich in cultural diversity. Taking the required precautions to ensure that you are well-prepared with the essential travel items is absolutely crucial if you want to have a pleasant and pleasurable holiday. In order to guarantee that you have an incredible journey to the Land of Smiles, this book has everything that you require, from the essential documentation to the safety and health items that you will require.

1. Travel Documents

Passport and Visa:

Determine when your passport will expire, as this is the first and most important stage in the process. Ensure that it will continue to be valid for a minimum of six months after the day that you intend to travel. In addition, check to see if a visa is required for your trip to Thailand, and if it is, make sure to get one in advance of your trip.

Travel Insurance:

The purchase of travel insurance that provides coverage for the entirety of the trip is an intelligent choice. In the event of an unexpected event, such as a medical emergency, a trip that is canceled, or lost luggage, this insurance coverage will cover all of these things. Make sure you always have a copy of your insurance information on you, as well as the phone numbers you need to call in case of an emergency.

Flight Tickets and Itinerary:

You can either keep electronic copies of your flight tickets and itinerary or print off printed copies of that information. For the purpose of check-ins as well as in the event that any unanticipated events take place, it may be beneficial to have this information stored in a location that is quickly accessible.

Accommodation Reservations:

It is essential that you maintain a record of your hotel arrangements, and this includes any emails that you receive as confirmation or references to your booking. Not only will this make the process of checking in more streamlined, but it will also offer you with a detailed itinerary for your stay overall.

2. Money and Banking

Thai Baht (Local Currency):

In spite of the fact that credit cards are frequently accepted, it is very important to have some Thai Baht on hand in order to make little transactions and to access establishments that might not accept cards. Banks and other approved currency exchange facilities are the ideal places to exchange currencies because they are the central locations.

Credit/Debit Cards:

I would appreciate it if you could tell your bank of your trip plan so that there are no problems with card transactions while you are away. Ensure that you always have a backup card on you and that you are aware of any fees that are associated with transactions that take place internationally.

Money Belt or Hidden Pouch:

You can protect your belongings from being stolen by wearing a money belt or a hidden bag, which is especially important in locations where there are a lot of vehicles. Through the utilization of this method, you will be able to effectively protect your money, credit cards, and other essential documents.

3. Health and Safety

Personal Medication and Prescriptions: Please make sure you bring a sufficient quantity of your normal meds, as well as any prescriptions that you might be taking at the time. You might want to think about carrying a simple first aid kit with you at all times. This kit has to have a variety of essential over-the-counter medications, including pain medicines, sticky bandages, and other essential items.

Insect Repellent: Because Thailand is located in a tropical climate, it is more likely that you will come across insects there. If you wish to protect yourself against mosquitoes and other insects, especially in rural or outdoor regions, it is essential to always have an efficient insect repellent on hand. This is especially true in situations where you are outside.

Use a sunscreen with a high sun protection factor (SPF) to shield your skin from the harsh rays of the tropical sun. It is recommended that you carry a sunscreen with a high sun protection factor (SPF) with you and that you apply it frequently, especially if you want to spend a few hours outside.

4. Clothing

Lightweight and Breathable Clothes: Thailand's weather is typically warm and muggy. Make sure you bring lightweight, breathable clothing to ensure comfort. Both cotton and linen fabrics are excellent choices.

Swimwear: Whether you plan to lounge on the gorgeous beaches or take a dip in the hotel pool, you must always remember to pack your swimsuit.

Comfortable Walking Shoes: Walking is a must when visiting Thailand, so make sure you pack appropriate walking shoes. Consider investing in a pair of shoes that are suitable for both visiting the city and taking walks in the woods.

Sandals or Flip-Flops: You should wear more casual footwear whether visiting markets or having a day at the beach. The best shoes to wear if you want to keep your feet cool are sandals or flip-flops.

Hat and Sunglasses: To protect your eyes from the sun's rays, put on a wide-brimmed hat and sunglasses. These supplies are really essential, especially for outdoor activities.

5. Electronics

Power adapter: Type A and Type C sockets in Thailand are used, and they have a standard voltage of 230V and frequency of 50Hz. To charge your electronics, remember to pack an appropriate power adaptor.

Smartphone and charger: A smartphone makes a convenient

travel companion. Maintaining connectivity and capturing lifelong memories can be achieved by installing practical travel applications and traveling with a charger.

Camera and Accessories: You can photograph Thailand's natural beauty if you have a camera that you can rely on. Don't forget to include any extra gear you might need, such extra memory cards, a camera case, and a tripod.

Carrying a portable charger or power bank can help you maintain the battery life of your electronic devices when you're out and about. When exploring for extended lengths of time, this is quite helpful.

6. Toiletries

Travel-sized Shampoo, Conditioner, and Soap: One excellent strategy to minimize the size of your toiletries pack is to include travel-sized versions of the products that are most essential to you. Furthermore, a lot of motels provide their visitors with basic toiletries.

Toothbrush and toothpaste: You should use your toothbrush and toothpaste to ensure that you are practicing proper oral hygiene. Space-saving solutions that are travel-sized are convenient because they require less room.

Hairbrush or Comb: To keep your hair looking neat, use a tiny brush or comb. When choosing the products for your hair care regimen, take the weather into account.

Items for personal hygiene:

Bring any supplies that are necessary for maintaining your personal hygiene, such sanitary products, along with you on your trip, along with any other goods you might need.

7. Travel Gear

Lightweight Backpack or Daypack: A lightweight backpack or daypack is essential for day travels and for carrying necessities. Check to see if it's comfortable and has enough room for your belongings.

Travel Pillow and Eye Mask: During long trips, the comfort and quality of your sleep can be greatly improved by using a travel pillow and an eye mask. Make sure you are rested and ready to explore when you arrive.

Travel Locks: Investing in travel locks is a terrific method to ensure the security of your belongings. Choose locks that have been approved by the Transportation Security Administration if you wish to pass security checks with ease.

Quick-dry Towel: Having a towel that dries fast is a smart idea, especially if you plan to visit the beach or engage in water-related activities. It forms a compact and dries swiftly.

8. Miscellaneous

Travel Guidebooks and Maps: Utilizing a travel guidebook or maps might enhance your vacation experience. These people have highly helpful insights on the local way of life, tourist destinations, and information.

Snorkeling Gear: If you plan to visit Thailand's coral reefs and islands, you may want to consider packing snorkeling gear. However, there are many of places that offer rental options.

Reusable Water Bottle:

Keeping a reusable water bottle with you will aid in your hydration. Refilling it as needed will help you cut down on the quantity of single-use plastic you use while also helping to preserve the environment.

Ziplock Bags: These bags come in a variety of uses, such as organizing small items in your luggage, storing snacks, and shielding electrical gadgets from dampness.

9. Clothing Considerations

Appropriate Clothing for Temples: When visiting temples and other places of worship, modest attire is appropriate. It is usually mandatory to wear long skirts or pants and sleeved shirts. Always have a thin scarf on hand in case you need further protection.

Lightweight Rain Jacket or Poncho: It is strongly advised that you pack a lightweight rain jacket or poncho for your trip during the rainy season. Keep everything dry and comfortable, especially in tropical areas where there are unexpected downpours.

10. Language and Communication

Simple Thai Phrases or Translation App: By being familiar with a few basic Thai terms, you can enhance your interactions with locals. Using a translation app is an additional choice for getting around language barriers.

Local SIM Card: To keep your connection going, get a local SIM card when you get there. They provide a range of reasonably priced options for calling and data, and they are conveniently accessible at the airport or local merchants.

11. Optional Items

Travel Umbrella: It's a good idea to be prepared with an umbrella in case of unexpected downpours. Compact umbrellas are handy to pack in your luggage when you're traveling.

Noise-canceling Headphones: You may want to consider packing noise-cancelling headphones if you want your travel experience to be more enjoyable, particularly on long flights. Turn off the noise around you and tune in to your favorite music or podcasts.

Entertainment:

Have a book, tablet, or e-reader with you so you can pass the time while you're not working. When entertainment of any kind is available, it could offer a much-needed break when traveling or on relaxing evenings.

Snacks for the Journey: It's crucial to pack snacks for your vacation, particularly if you have any dietary restrictions or preferences. It can be comforting to have familiar snacks with you when traveling.

Make sure you have packed everything you'll need and have done a lot of planning in order to guarantee a successful and enjoyable holiday to Thailand. Make sure that this checklist is customized to your own needs and preferences, then prepare to be enthralled by the beauty and culture of this intriguing Southeast Asian destination.

Chapter 2:
Must Visit Places In Thailand

Thailand, often known as the "Land of Smiles," is a popular travel destination because of its vibrant modern cities, stunning landscapes, and rich cultural heritage. Thailand offers a vast array of experiences for travelers of all stripes, ranging from bustling markets to serene temples, unspoiled beaches to lush jungles, and all points in between. We'll look at some of the most significant places in Southeast Asia in this chapter, which is sure to enthrall you with their stunning landscapes and rich cultural histories.

Bangkok: The Vibrant Capital

Bangkok, Thailand's bustling capital, is a must-see destination for any traveler visiting the country. Bangkok is a thriving metropolis that never stops evolving and a city that skillfully blends modernization and tradition. The contrast between the grand structures, exquisite temples, and bustling street markets makes for an intriguing visit.

Wat Phra Kaew and the Grand Palace

Situated in the heart of Bangkok, the Grand Palace is a magnificent building that has been the official residence of the Thai Kings for almost 200 years. On the grounds of the palace structures is where you will find Wat Phra Kaew, commonly known as the Temple of the Emerald Buddha. There is a highly revered little statue of Buddha inside the temple that was carved out of a single jade block. Because of its intricate construction, vivid colors, and exquisite workmanship, this place should not be missed by anyone interested in Thai history and culture.

What Arun

Wat Arun, also called the Temple of Dawn, will be encountered as you cross the Chao Phraya River. With its riverbank setting, which is renowned for its spectacular beauty, and its distinctive spires that are covered with dazzling ceramic designs, Wat Arun is a captivating sight, especially when viewed at sunrise or sunset. Reaching the peak of the mountain offers amazing views of the city, making it a popular spot for both tourists and locals.

Weekend Market at Chatuchak

For those seeking an alternative kind of adventure, the Chatuchak Weekend Market is a shoppers' dream come true. There are more than 8,000 vendors offering a vast array of products at this massive market, from exotic pets and delicious street food to local handicrafts and vintage clothing. An excess of senses is present. Here, visitors may experience the local way of life and buy unique souvenirs to bring back home.

Chiang Mai: The North's Cultural Jewel

The city of Chiang Mai is well-known for its historic temples, vibrant night markets, and the surrounding scenic splendor. Situated in the undulating terrain of Northern Thailand, this city boasts an extensive cultural history.

Doi Suthep

On top of a mountain with a view of Chiang Mai sits a revered temple known as Wat Phra That Doi Suthep. There is an intriguing legend connected to this temple. The temple, a hallowed site of pilgrimage, is renowned for its exquisitely adorned architecture and golden chedi. Travelers can reach the temple by taking a scenic drive along the meandering mountain roads or by climbing the Naga staircase. These are two easily available possibilities.

Temples and the Old City

Chiang Mai's Old City is a charming district completely surrounded by ancient walls and a moat. The several temples situated within its confines are all completely distinct in terms of their architectural style and historical background. Some of the religious and historical riches in this city are Wat Chedi Luang, Wat Phra Singh, and Wat Suan Dok, to name just a few.

Chiang Mai Night Bazaar As soon as the sun sets, Chiang Mai becomes a hive of activity with the opening of the Night Bazaar. Customers can choose from an extensive selection of handicrafts, fabrics, and regional specialties at this bustling market. This place is great for learning about the local way of life. Enjoy some delicious street cuisine, some traditional performances, and the local culture.

Phuket: Tropical Paradise in the Andaman Sea

If you are searching for beaches with turquoise oceans and lots of sunlight, Phuket, Thailand is the place to go. The biggest island in the nation, Phuket, is well-known for both its exciting nightlife and stunning natural beauty.

Patong Shoreline

The epicenter of Phuket's vibrant atmosphere is Patong Beach. Its long stretch of golden sand and array of water sports make it the perfect spot for activities that mix excitement and relaxation. There's always something going on along the beach because of the restaurants, bars, and businesses that line the perimeter of the beach.

Islands of Phi Phi

A tropical paradise known for its picture-perfect scenery is the Phi Phi Islands. From Phuket, they are only a short boat trip away. Visitors can enjoy fantastic opportunities to partake in activities like snorkeling, diving, and just soaking up the breathtaking beauty on both Phi Phi Don and Phi Phi Leh. The clear waters, striking coral reefs, and limestone cliffs that define these islands.

Large Buddha

Soaring to a height of 45 meters, the Big Buddha is among Phuket's most identifiable landmarks. Perched atop Nakkerd Hill, the imposing monument offers stunning views of the island's surrounds and the Andaman Sea. This location also features a prayer hall and a smaller golden Buddha, both of which contribute to the contemplative ambiance.

Ayutthaya: Historical Marvels

More than 400 years after Ayutthaya was the second capital of the Siamese Kingdom, the city is now listed as a UNESCO World Heritage Site. It displays relics from a time when the world was different, acting as a treasure trove for archaeologists today.

Park Ayutthaya Historical

The Ayutthaya Historical Park contains a great deal of interesting ruins. These remains, which are home to statues, palaces, and temples, provide a glimpse into the opulence of the ancient dynasty. Wat Mahathat, which is distinguished by the fabled Buddha head entwined in a banyan tree's roots, is a very fascinating sight. Renting a bicycle and embarking on an expedition through the expansive park is a popular and enjoyable way to take in the historical attractions of the area.

Bang Pa-In Royal Palace

Bang Pa-In Royal Palace is a spectacular complex that served as the summer retreat for the Thai monarchs, while being only a short distance from Ayutthaya. The palace is home to a wide range of architectural designs, including those influenced by European, Thai, and Chinese architecture. Visitors can enjoy strolling through beautifully manicured gardens, exploring grand pavilions, and marveling at the intricate constructions that pay homage to the nation's imperial past.

Krabi: Nature's Playground

Situated on the Andaman Sea, Krabi is a popular tourist destination because of its stunning limestone cliffs, pristine waters, and fascinating islands. It is a haven for those who love the outdoors and discovering new things.

Beach Railay

Towering limestone cliffs surround Railay Beach, making it an ideal site for rock climbers and beachgoers both. However, access to the beach is limited to boats. It is a spot that simply must be seen because of the unspoiled sand, the extraordinarily pure waters, and the gorgeous surrounds. Rock climbing schools provide an opportunity for climbers of all ability levels to ascend the steep cliffs that define the area.

Tour to Four Islands

Taking the Four Islands Tour is a well-liked method of discovering the splendor of the Krabi archipelago. Typically, the tour stops at Chicken Island, Tup Island, Poda Island, and Phra Nang Cave Beach. Every island has its own special qualities, such as breathtaking coral reefs or quiet lagoons, offering a variety of experiences in a single trip.

Emerald Pool and Thung Teao Forest Natural Park

The well-known Emerald Pool, which offers guests a tranquil getaway into nature, is located in Thung Teao Forest Natural Park. Rich in minerals, the warm waters of the pool offer a soothing and rejuvenating experience. The pool's waters are encircled by dense foliage. The fact that the majestic Tham Klang cave is accessible with a quick walk through the jungle adds an extra element of excitement to the adventure.

Sukhothai: Birthplace of Thai Civilization

Sukhothai, the site of Thailand's first capital, is crucial to comprehending both the early history and the emergence of the nation's culture. The Sukhothai Historical Park is a UNESCO World Heritage Site, with the aim of conserving the remnants of this ancient city.

Park Sukhothai Historical

The Sukhothai Historical Park is an outdoor museum that showcases the remarkably preserved remnants of 13th-century temples, palaces, and sculptures. Thailand is where the park is situated. There are several zones inside the park, and each has its own unique blend of historically significant elements and architectural styles. The stupas of Wat Mahathat shaped like lotus buds and the serene atmosphere at Wat Si Chum, which is home to a large Buddha statue, are two of the attractions.

National Museum at Ramkhamhaeng

To have a deeper understanding of Sukhothai history, it is highly recommended that one visit the Ramkhamhaeng National Museum. The museum houses an assemblage of antiquities, sculptures, and historical displays that narrate the history of the area from its inception to the present. With this, one can learn a great deal about Sukhothai's creative and cultural achievements.

Pai: Tranquil Haven in the Mountains

The tiny town of Pai, which is found in the northern Thai highlands, is well-known for its relaxed atmosphere, gorgeous surroundings, and vibrant arts scene.

Pai Canyon

Amazing panoramic views of the surrounding mountains and valleys may be seen from the Pai Canyon, also known as Kong Lan. Taking advantage of the sheer cliffs and narrow ridges makes for an incredible climb, especially in the morning or evening. The natural beauty and quiet of the canyon attract tourists seeking a peaceful getaway from the bustle of the big cities.

Waterfalls and Hot Springs

Naturally occurring hot springs and waterfalls surround the town of Pai, providing opportunities for both adventure and relaxation. In the middle of lush surroundings, the Pong Dueat Hot Springs offer visitors a tranquil experience, and the Mo Paeng Waterfall entices them to dip in its cool pools. These unspoiled natural gems are wonderful illustrations of the unspoiled splendor of the landscapes in Northern Thailand.

Thailand's allure is found not only in its magnificent scenery but also in the warmth of its people, the richness of its culture, and the range of activities it offers. Some of the places that add to Thailand's unique charm are the historic ruins of Ayutthaya, the serene beaches of Phuket, the bustling streets of Bangkok, and the highland panoramas of Chiang Mai and Pai.

This chapter has just begun to scratch the surface of the treasures that await visitors to the Land of Smiles. For those who are lucky enough to venture into its enchanted domains, Thailand extends a warm welcome, eager to share its treasures and make lifelong memories. Thailand is ready to welcome you whether you're an adventure seeker, a history buff, a beach lover, or you're just searching for a quiet getaway.

Chapter 3: Itineraries

Thailand is a popular travel destination because of its enticing charm. It is a nation renowned for its vibrant culture, breathtaking scenery, and kind hospitality. As we delve deeper into the center of this Southeast Asian treasure, our itinerary takes shape like a tapestry of encounters. It seamlessly combines the many landscapes, the extensive history, and the unique blend of modernism and tradition that define Thailand.

Day 1: Arrival in Bangkok - A City of Contrasts

Our trip begins in Bangkok, the vibrant capital city, where modern skyscrapers and historic temples coexist in an amazing contrast that is fascinating to observe. The aroma of Thai orchids greets us as soon as we arrive at Suvarnabhumi Airport, setting the mood for the sensory experience that lies ahead.

Following our arrival, we will embark on a river cruise down the Chao Phraya River after checking into a hotel in a convenient area. Sailing past the well-known Wat Arun temple, glowing against the night sky, allows us to witness the harmonious fusion of historic building design with modern cityscape. We are introduced to the magnificent flavors of Thai cuisine over supper aboard the ship, which is a delicious blend of sweet, sour, salty, and spicy sensations.

Day 2: Temples and Traditions - A Cultural Odyssey

We will explore the cultural gems that Bangkok has to offer on our second day here. Our first destination will be the majestic Grand Palace, which houses the renowned Emerald Buddha. The murals' vibrant colors and the intricate details of the architecture together tell a story about the royal dynasty of Thailand.

After that, we go to Wat Pho, the site of the massive Buddha lying in a reclining posture. The temple complex offers instruction in the traditional Thai massage technique in addition to being a site of immense spiritual significance. After an invigorating practice, we treat ourselves to a local dinner where we indulge in the delectable fragrances of Pad Thai and Tom Yum soup.

We take an afternoon tour to see Bangkok's bustling markets, which includes the Chatuchak Weekend Market. This market offers everything from fragrant spices to handcrafted handicrafts, making it a genuine treasure trove of Thai culture. We head to a traditional Thai dance performance as the day comes to an end. Storytelling from Thai mythology and tradition is combined with the elegance of classical dance.

Day 3: Chiang Mai - The Rose of the North

We take a flight to Chiang Mai, Thailand's cultural capital, to escape the buzzing busyness of Bangkok. This city exudes a tranquil charm because it is surrounded by mist-covered mountains. We will now start our adventure in the Old City, which is surrounded by ancient walls and home to numerous temples like Wat Chedi Luang and Wat Phra Singh.

We spend the evening exploring the vibrant Night Bazaar, which is a mixture of colors and sounds. We sample some of the regional specialties, like Khao Soi, a popular noodle soup in northern Thailand, and watch some traditional Lanna dance performances while meandering through the market.

Day 4: Elephants and Hill Tribes - Connecting with Nature

It is hard to travel to Thailand and not be able to appreciate the magnificent natural surroundings of the nation. We visit an ethical elephant sanctuary as part of our day trip, where we can interact with these gentle giants and learn about the conservation efforts being made. A strong bond with the natural environment is developed and lifelong memories are made while bathing and feeding the elephants.

In the afternoon, we travel up into the hills to see a Karen Long Neck Tribe village. Through this cross-cultural interaction, the traditions and way of life of the indigenous people are revealed, leading to a greater understanding. After a peaceful visit to the Doi Suthep Temple, perched on a mountain and offering stunning views of Chiang Mai, the day draws to an end.

Day 5: Krabi - Island Paradise Beckons

The stunning province of Krabi, which is situated on Thailand's southeast coast, is where we're going next. The stunning islands, turquoise oceans, and limestone cliffs in this region are well-known. We arrive in Ao Nang, a beach town that serves as our point of entry into the Andaman Sea, after a short flight.

In the evening, we boarded a long-tail boat to explore the well-known Four Islands, which are home to well-known locations including Phra Nang Cave Beach and Tup Island. A supper on the beach is picture-perfect, with the shimmering waters and golden sunsets creating the ideal backdrop.

Day 6: Railay Beach and Adventure

We take a quick boat ride to Railay Beach, a beachgoer's paradise and a rock climber's paradise. We spend the day exploring the limestone caverns and secret lagoons buried around the area before trying our hand at rock climbing or relaxing with a spa treatment.

Throughout the evening, Fire Dancers perform on the beach as

Railay is converted into a mysterious place. Eating a seafood feast at one of the restaurants that are directly on the beach is the perfect way to end our excursion along the coast.

Day 7: Phuket - The Pearl of the Andaman

Phuket, the biggest island in Thailand, is the last stop on our itinerary. We first take a drive through some breathtaking scenery before seeing the old town, which is renowned for its vibrant street art and Sino-Portuguese architecture. The afternoon is dedicated to lounging on the popular Patong Beach, where the vibrant mood contrasts sharply with the serene serenity of the surroundings.

We have a farewell dinner at a restaurant on the shore in the evening. We pause during this meal to think back on the wonderful encounters and memories we have made while traveling around Thailand.

We are bidding our goodbyes to the Land of Smiles, and the warmth of the Thai people's hospitality, the breathtaking scenery, and the depth of their culture are all bursting in our hearts. Every visitor to Thailand departs with a lingering impression that begs them to come back and take in even more of the wonders of the nation. Thailand's many offerings create a lasting impression on that spirit.

Chapter 4:
Best Restaurants and Cuisine

A gastronomic adventure that is as rich and varied as the nation's cultural tapestry can be found in Thailand. Thailand is well-known for its lively street cuisine, fragrant spices, and unusual flavors. The busy marketplaces of Bangkok and the tranquil coastal towns each offer their own one-of-a-kind dining experiences, and every region of the country offers something different. In this chapter, we take a look at some of the most well-known restaurants and cuisines in Thailand. We highlight the mouthwatering meals that have contributed to the widespread popularity of Thai cuisine around the world.

Bangkok's Street Food Extravaganza

Those who are passionate about food will find that the streets of Bangkok are a veritable feast for the senses. The street food culture of the city is a vivid kaleidoscope of flavors, smells, and colors that are just waiting to be tasted by curious individuals. A tantalizing culinary symphony is created as we make our way through the crowded marketplaces and the small alleys to reach our destination. The colorful displays of ingredients, the sound of woks sizzling, and the aromas of meats being grilled all contribute to the creation of this symphony.

- Pad Thai Thip Samai, a well-known restaurant, has been working to perfect the art of pad thai ever since it opened its doors in 1966. The restaurant is renowned for having the "Best Pad Thai in Bangkok," and it has once again demonstrated that it is deserving of this moniker. Using enormous woks, this dish was cooked to perfection, bringing together flavors of sour, sweet, and salty in perfect harmony with one another.
- Wherever You Are: Som Tum Der is a restaurant that specializes in Som Tum, which is also known as green papaya salad. It is a veritable haven for individuals who are looking for the ideal combination of flavors that are sour, spicy, and refreshing. The menu also features a selection of additional Isaan dishes, providing customers with a genuine flavor of the cuisine of the northeastern region of Thailand.
- To quote Jay Fai: It is highly recommended that you visit Jay Fai, a streetside cafe that has been awarded a Michelin star, if you are looking for a sophisticated approach to street food. In addition to being well-known for its drunken noodles and crab omelets, it is also renowned for its flawless combination of the attraction of street food and the brilliance of fine dining.

Exploring Northern Flavors in Chiang Mai

Chiang Mai, which is considered to be the cultural center of Thailand, is beginning to develop a culinary scene that is beginning to take on a distinct flavor that is typical of northern Thailand. The Lanna culture, which is so prevalent in this region, has inspired the abundance of food that can be found at the traditional eateries and local markets of this region. These establishments offer an incredible variety of food.

- Huen Muan Jai is a restaurant that provides a dining experience that is genuine to the Lanna culture. It is located in the center of the Old City. Sai Ua, a savory northern Thai sausage, and Khao Soi, a coconut curry noodle soup, are two examples of meals that are featured on the menu. Both of these dishes highlight the rich culinary legacy that is associated with the region.
- Khao Soi Khun Yai: The exceptional Khao Soi at Khao Soi Khun Yai, which is a small modest restaurant that has established a cult following, is frequently considered to be among the best in the world. A symphony of flavors and textures can be found in this dish, which is made up of egg noodles that are drenched in a thick coconut curry sauce. After that, a selection of protein and noodles that have been crisped up are added to the dish.
- If you want to try chicken that has been roasted to perfection, Cherng Doi Roast Chicken is the location that the locals recommend the most time and time again. It is a monument to the simplicity and perfection of northern Thai cuisine that the chicken, which is both wonderful and exquisite, comes with a variety of dipping sauces.

Coastal Culinary Adventures in Krabi

As we make our way toward the seaside district of Krabi, the culinary scene begins to change to mirror the bounty of the ocean surrounding us. Fresh fish, tropical fruits, and aromatic herbs are the primary components that form the foundation of the cuisine of the region.

- Krua Thara: Situated directly next to the beach, Krua Thara serves up a seafood feast with a view. Some of the most delectable Andaman Sea regional specialties, like grilled

prawns and fish cooked in lime sauce, are offered on the menu. At Krua Thara, the sunset meals are meant to be a sensory experience, and the sound of the waves perfectly matches the mouthwatering fare provided.
- Lae Lay Grill: For a romantic seafood dinner, the Lae Lay Grill, which is built on a cliff overlooking the ocean, is the perfect setting. Customers can taste the flavors that naturally arise from the ocean by choosing from a variety of dipping sauces that are served with grilled fish, prawns, and lobster.
- Chalita Cafe & Restaurant: Offering a wide selection of dishes that are typical of southern Thai cuisine, Chalita Cafe & Restaurant has a varied menu. These recipes include unique seafood meals, fiery curries, and delicious stir-fries. This is the perfect location to relax and savor the delicacies that are distinctive to the coast because of the laid-back attitude.

Phuket's Fusion of Flavors

Our journey across the world of cuisine comes to a conclusion in Phuket, where a unique combination of Thai, Chinese, and Malay influences results in a flavorful confluence that is sure to satisfy your taste buds. The culinary scene in Phuket is designed to accommodate a diverse range of preferences, with options ranging from lively street cuisine to luxury dining venues.

- Suay Restaurant: Located in Old Phuket Town, Suay Restaurant serves creative cuisine that includes dishes like Soft Shell Crab with Tamarind Sauce and Massaman Curry Pizza. The restaurant combines traditional cuisine with modern décor. The fusion of flavors and textures this restaurant delivers makes it a hallmark in Phuket's culinary scene.
- Restaurant Kaab Gluay: Located in Rawai Beach, this eatery is a well-kept secret and well-known for its

authentic southern Thai food. The menu features traditional items like Stir-Fried Blue Crab with Curry Powder and Gaeng Som Pla, a fish curry with a sour and spicy taste. The strong, fragrant qualities that define the area are emphasized in these recipes.
- Raya Restaurant: Having been in business for almost 20 years, the Raya Restaurant is a well-known establishment in Phuket. Meals that are regarded as typical of Phuket can be found on its menu. Raya Restaurant is dedicated to maintaining the island's culinary heritage, which includes specialties like Moo Hong and Mee Hokkien, which is akin to Hokkien noodles (similar to braised pig belly).

Thai Desserts and Sweet Endings

It would be impossible to conduct a comprehensive investigation of Thai cuisine without first trying some of the several delectable desserts that are produced in the country. Desserts from Thailand, such as the well-known Mango Sticky Rice and the elaborate and colorful Kanom Chan, which is made with a variety of ingredients, are a celebration of flavors and textures.

- Mango Tango: Mango Tango elevates the unremarkable meal of mango sticky rice to the status of an art form. It is a dessert paradise located in Bangkok. A harmonious combination of fresh mangoes, sweet sticky rice, and coconut milk creates a delightful symphony that delights the senses.
- Thong Kee Dessert: If you're searching for a traditional Thai dessert experience, Thong Kee Dessert in Chiang Mai offers a variety of delicious treats, such as an assortment of Khanom Buang, which are crisp pancakes filled with cream, and Lod Chong (green noodles in coconut milk).
- Boon Sap Thai Desserts: For both locals and tourists alike, Boon Sap Thai Desserts is a popular location in Phuket. The Khanom Chan, a rainbow, exquisitely layered dessert,

is one of the many traditional Thai desserts that are offered on the menu.

Thai Street Drinks - Cool Refreshments for Every Palate

As a result of its tropical climate, Thailand has a significant demand for beverages that are refreshing, and the culture of street drinks in the country is just as diversified as the cuisine scene. A wide variety of beverages, ranging from the classic Thai iced tea to the unique fruit smoothies, are available to choose from.

- Cha Yen (Thai Iced Tea): Blended with condensed milk, Cha Yen is a sweet and creamy iced tea. It's a readily accessible, well-liked street beverage. It is a well-liked option for those looking to beat the heat because of its tasty flavor and orange hue.
- Nam Manao (Lime Soda): Nam Manao is a hot beverage that perfectly complements the bold tastes of Thai food. It's a delicious drink that consists of sugar, soda water, and lime juice.
- Tropical Fruit Shakes: Buying a tropical fruit shake from one of the numerous street vendors spread throughout Thailand will allow you to savor the tastes of mango, pineapple, watermelon, and other tropical fruits. These refreshing, vibrant drinks are the perfect after-work pick me up for a long day of research.

Thailand's food offers an amazing symphony of tastes, textures, and fragrances that tantalize the senses. Every location offers a unique gastronomic experience, from the bustling street markets in Bangkok to the tranquil villages by the sea. Thailand's diverse cuisine reflects the country's cultural diversity and the creativity of its chefs, whether you're enjoying the world-famous Pad Thai in the heart of the capital city or eating on fresh seafood by the Andaman Sea. The recollections of these wonderful sensations cling to one's palate as one's journey through Thailand's culinary wonders comes to an end, enticing every traveler to return to the Land of Smiles for yet another culinary exploration.

Chapter 5:
Accommodations in Thailand

As a result of its attractive combination of rich cultural diversity, breathtaking scenery, and friendly people, Thailand has become a popular tourism destination. As more and more tourists travel to various regions of this Southeast Asian treasure, the question of where to stay is becoming an increasingly important component of the conversation. Within the scope of this chapter, we shall investigate the wide variety of hotel options that are accessible in Thailand. All of these options are suitable for a wide range of interests and spending levels.

1. **Luxury Retreats: Indulgence Redefined**

The warm hospitality that is synonymous with Thailand is reflected by the country's magnificent resorts and five-star hotels, which are well-known throughout the world. There is a wide range of choices accessible, ranging from the teeming metropolis of Bangkok to the tranquil islands of Koh Samui and Phuket in Thailand. There are a number of reputable establishments, such as the Amanpuri in Phuket and the Mandarin Oriental in Bangkok, that offer the ideal atmosphere for an elegant stay by combining the most luxurious amenities with the allure of traditional Thai culture.

Typically extending across verdant landscapes, these luxurious vacation spots provide a variety of amenities, including wellness centers, private villas, and individualized services. It is possible that these lodgings will offer a cozy and exclusive hideaway for those individuals who are looking for an experience that cannot be matched by anything else.

2. Charming Boutique Stays: Personalized Elegance

Visitors to Thailand who are looking for an alternative to the lavishness of luxury resorts will find that boutique hotels provide a more personal and intimate experience than luxury resorts. The beauty of the modern period and the allure of the local culture are able to be successfully combined by these establishments, regardless of whether they are located along the tranquil coasts of Hua Hin or in the culturally bustling city of Chiang Mai.

Customers staying in boutique hotels are provided with a one-of-a-kind experience, which frequently highlights the creative and design capabilities of the community that surrounds the hotel. These accommodations are an excellent option for vacationers who are looking for a more immersive and one-of-a-kind experience throughout their stay. This is because of the emphasis placed on customized care and attention to detail.

3. Seaside Escapes: Beachfront Resorts

An large variety of beachfront resorts can be found along the coast of Thailand, many of them are distinguished by the fact that their beaches are in pristine condition. There are resorts in places like Phuket, Krabi, and Koh Samui that provide you with beautiful lodgings in addition to providing you with direct access to the beaches that are bathed in sunlight. These businesses offer to a wide variety of preferences, ranging from resorts that are suitable for families and have water parks to hideaways that are reserved exclusively for adults.

Resorts located on the beach typically offer a variety of amenities, including panoramic views, infinity pools, and the ability to participate in a variety of water activities, in addition to providing pleasant lodgings. What makes them so appealing to people is this very thing. These coastal villas provide a fantastic location for a visit that will be remembered and cherished for the rest of one's life. They are perfect for a vacation with your significant other or with your family.

4. **Heritage Homestays: Immersed in Thai Culture**

The heritage homestays in Thailand provide a one-of-a-kind chance for individuals who have an insatiable curiosity about the country's rich history. One can find these kind of hotel alternatives in places like Ayutthaya and Sukhothai, and they are typically housed in structures that are considered to be historic. The opportunity to journey back in time while still taking advantage of modern conveniences is provided to guests who visit these establishments.

Some of the distinguishing characteristics of heritage hotels are the presence of vintage furnishings, tranquil courtyards that are on exhibit, and traditional Thai architecture. Not only do these accommodations provide a place to relax, but they also give guests the opportunity to completely submerge themselves in the culture of the area. In addition, some of these hotels offer guided excursions of the historical places that are located in the surrounding area.

5. **Eco-Friendly Havens: Sustainable Retreats**

In accordance with the global trend toward eco-friendly travel, environmentally friendly accommodations are becoming more and more common in Thailand. Situated amidst natural wonders like Khao Sok National Park and Chiang Rai, these resorts provide a harmonic blend of luxury and environmental responsibility.

Eco-friendly accommodations in Thailand prioritize eco-friendly practices such as trash minimization, energy efficiency, and assistance for local groups engaged in environmental conservation. These refuges ensure a guilt-free and revitalizing experience, which makes them perfect for travelers hoping to forge a deeper bond with nature.

6. **Urban Oases: City Hotels**

Thailand's cities are humming with activity, and city hotels provide a comfortable and convenient base from which to explore the region. Bangkok, Chiang Mai, and Pattaya provide a multitude of options, from budget-friendly hotels to more luxurious ones.

City hotels serve both leisure and business guests, and they are situated near cultural attractions, retail areas, and exciting entertainment venues. These lodgings are appropriate for people who want to experience the dynamic urban life that Thailand has to offer because of the seamless integration of comfort and ease.

7. **Budget-Friendly Hideouts: Hostels and Guesthouses**

Thailand offers a wide range of reasonably priced lodging options, such as guesthouses and hostels, to meet the demands of tourists on a low budget. There are many of reasonably priced options to choose from, from the popular Khao San Road in Bangkok to the relaxed atmosphere of Pai in the north.

Apart from promoting social interaction among travelers, these lodgings also establish a lively atmosphere where cost-conscious explorers may share their experiences and provide guidance to one other. Hostels and guesthouses are not only affordable but often provide an entry point into the local history and culture, as well as the chance to make lifelong friendships with other tourists.

Thailand's accommodations are a mosaic of hospitality, catering to a broad range of budgets and interests. Whatever one's preference—a luxurious getaway, an individualized, private encounter, or the height of luxury—hotel Thailand's options provide an experience that will never be forgotten.

It is crucial to think about the unique qualities that every kind of accommodation has to offer when you are preparing to travel through Thailand. Let the vibrant energy of the Land of Smiles guide you to the best lodging option for your tour. In addition to providing a place to stay, Thailand's accommodations offer to be an integral part of the rich tapestry that makes every visit to this amazing destination truly unique. Whether you are visiting one of the nation's busy cities or one of its serene islands, this is true.

Chapter 6:
Cultural Activities in Thailand

Thailand has a lot to offer, more than just its stunning scenery and bustling towns, including a rich cultural past that enthralls visitors. In this chapter, we will explore the wide range of cultural activities that Thailand has to offer. We'll give you a peek of the customs, artwork, and ceremonies that truly set this Southeast Asian country apart.

Temple Discovery: Hallowed Treasures

Thailand is home to some of the most beautiful temples on the planet. Thailand has deeply rooted cultural and spiritual traditions, which are honored at each of these temples. From the well-known Wat Arun in Bangkok to the ancient capital of Ayutthaya, where temples like Wat Phra Si Sanphet dominate the landscape with their intimidating quiet, temple exploring is an essential cultural activity that can be found all around Thailand.

The ornate architecture, vibrant murals, and golden spires that characterize Thai temples are available for viewing by guests. One can obtain a deeper knowledge of the spiritual practices that have been essential to the development of Thai culture over several centuries by participating in a traditional Buddhist ceremony or going on a guided temple tour.

Traditional Thai Dancing: Style in Motion

Traditional Thai dancing is a unique art form that showcases the grace and sophistication inherent in Thai culture. Events like the Khon dance performance, which is distinguished by its elaborate costumes and superb choreography, provide an insight into the nation's historical narratives.

Tourists can either attend cultural events conducted in major towns or visit cultural institutes like the Thailand Cultural Centre in Bangkok to witness these captivating performances. Several places even offer dancing lessons, allowing visitors to try their hand (or feet) at the captivating moves that are distinctive to Thai dance.

Muay Thai: The Eight-Legged Art

In addition to being a sport, muay thai has a deep cultural significance in Thailand. It is well known as the "Art of Eight Limbs," and many people practice it. One excellent approach for tourists to understand the skill and dedication needed to learn Muay Thai is to see a live match. Stadiums are regularly used to host fights where professional fighters showcase their skills in locations like Bangkok and Chiang Mai.

To provide visitors a more immersive experience, a lot of training camps offers the chance to learn the basics of Muay Thai. Attending training sessions provides participants with more than just a physical workout; they also learn about the discipline and cultural significance of this highly renowned martial art.

Floating Markets: A Flavorful Symphony

You'll embark on a sensory-exciting cultural journey as you explore Thailand's floating markets. Markets like Damnoen Saduak, in Bangkok, and Amphawa, in Samut Songkhram, offer a vibrant selection of fresh vegetables, handicrafts from the area, and delicious street food. Navigating the crowded rivers in a traditional long-tail boat is an adventure in and of itself.

These unique marketplaces provide guests the chance to mingle with neighborhood vendors, sample local cuisine, and see how people go about their daily lives. Floating markets not only provide an insight into Thailand's diverse gastronomic offerings, but they also underscore the importance of waterways in fostering local commerce.

Classes in Traditional Thai Cooking: Culinary Artistry

Thai cuisine has gained popularity all over the world thanks to its robust flavors and aromatic spices. Students can get practical knowledge in the technique of producing Thai delicacies by taking part in a workshop that teaches traditional Thai cuisine. There are many different types of classroom environments available to students, from the bustle of big cities like Bangkok to the peace and quiet of rural places.

While participating in these programs, participants will learn how to prepare popular dishes including Pad Thai, Tom Yum Goong, and Green Curry. Often, a visit to the nearby market to buy fresh ingredients is included in the lecture schedule. This enables students to comprehend the importance of each ingredient in Thai cuisine on a deeper level.

Songkran Festival: An Amazing Water Festival

The Thai New Year, or Songkran, is celebrated with great joy and fervor around the middle of April. The water fights that happen around the nation are among the most thrilling parts of this festival. These battles are intended to symbolize both the close of the previous year and the start of the current one.

As both locals and visitors partake in the water-splashing fun that these festivals necessitate, taking part in Songkran offers a unique cultural experience. Not only does the Songkran event feature water battles, but it also features customary rituals, parades, and self-improvement activities.

Meetings with Hill Tribes: Cultural Variety in Northern Thailand

The northern region of Thailand is home to several hill tribes, each with their unique customs, attire, and languages. Traveling to see these tribes—the Karen, Hmong, or Akha, for example—will provide you with the unique chance to encounter Thailand's highland cultures' diversity of cultures all at once.

It is possible for guests to stay in the houses of hill tribes, participate in customary celebrations, and learn about the unique arts and rituals of each of these communities. Beyond the more popular travel spots in Thailand's south and center, this extensive tour offers a deeper understanding of the country's many cultural offerings.

People that engage in Thailand's cultural events present a picture that is knitted together with tradition, spirituality, and artistic expression. Whether it's touring historic temples, taking part in traditional dancing, or indulging in delectable cuisine, every activity offers a window into the soul and heart of the Land of Smiles.

Seize the chance to interact with the people, absorb knowledge from customs that have existed for hundreds of years, and get fully enmeshed in the vibrant fabric that makes Thailand a destination unlike any other. You'll be able to maximize your cultural exploration of Thailand by doing this. These cultural activities will enrich your travel experience and leave you with lasting memories of the cultural treasures that set this captivating Southeast Asian country apart while you were there.

Chapter 7:
Nightlife And Festivals In Thailand

Different facets of Thailand come to life as the sun sets over its magnificent landscape. In Thailand, one can engage in a diverse range of activities following dusk, from vibrant festival displays to the throbbing sounds of nightlife across the nation. We will explore the vibrant nightlife scene in this chapter, along with the captivating events that add to the lively and joyous atmosphere that permeates the nation.

Extravaganza of Nightlife: From Rooftop Bars to Street Markets

Street Markets and Food Havens: Thailand's bustling street markets come alive at night, offering a vibrant and delectable evening experience. Cities like Bangkok and Chiang Mai come to life with the sizzle of street food vendors, the enticing fragrances, and the bustle of the environment as locals and visitors explore the night markets with excitement. Famous locations like Chiang Mai Night Bazaar and Bangkok's Khao San Road are well-known for their vibrant atmosphere, street entertainers, and an extensive selection of delectable Thai cuisine.

b. Rooftop Bars and Skyline Soirees: Thailand is a great place for those seeking a more upscale nightlife experience because of the abundance of rooftop bars that provide stunning views of the city skylines. Bangkok is particularly well-known for its culture of rooftop bars. There are places with a classy ambiance and expansive city views, like the Sky Bar at the Lebua State Tower and the Vertigo and Moon Bar at the Banyan Tree Hotel. The sensation of enjoying a martini outside while gazing up at the city lights is among the most recognizable images of Thai nightlife.

Full Moon Parties: Koh Phangan Beachside Celebrations

People from all over the globe have praised the Full Moon Party, an iconic event that happens in Koh Phangan. Every month, Haad Rin Beach is converted into a vibrant dance floor for a much-anticipated event on the evening of the full moon. There's an all-night beach party with fire dancers, electronic music, and a vibrant atmosphere. Thousands of people attend the celebration, both residents and tourists.

Thailand has established itself as a destination for nightlife, as demonstrated by the fact that partygoers travel from all over the world to attend the Full Moon Party. While Koh Phangan is most often linked with the Full Moon Party, other islands also host events that are strikingly similar and provide a unique and amazing evening experience.

Lanterns and River Offerings at Loy Krathong

Loy Krathong is one of Thailand's most lovely holidays, which takes place in November each year. Originating in Thai cultural and religious traditions, this celebration features a beautiful display of floating lights and offerings made in the river. Locals and tourists alike gather around rivers and other bodies of water to release krathongs, which are decorative floats made from banana leaves, flowers, and candles. The releasing of krathongs represents the banishing of bad energy.

The celebration will also feature traditional dance performances, parades, and cultural events. When Loy Krathong and the Yi Peng Lantern Festival coincide in Chiang Mai, the result is a breathtaking display of lanterns lighting the night sky.

Songkran Festival: Battles with Water and New Starts

The Thai New Year, or Songkran, is a celebration that takes place in April and is well-known for its lively and joyful vibe. Everywhere in the nation, water wars occur, and they are well-known for being iconic. These battles stand for the welcoming of the new year and the purging of the old one! Turning the streets into a water cannon and water balloon fight scene and having a wonderful time splashing around creates a happy and celebratory atmosphere.

The Songkran event includes water fights as well as traditional rites, parades, and activities like making merit. The event provides an unparalleled chance for locals and visitors to come together in a spirit of celebration and camaraderie.

Phi Ta Khon: Costumes and Joy in Loei

The Phi Ta Khon Festival is a celebration held in the town of Dan Sai, in the province of Loei. This holiday combines religious customs with fun activities, making it a colorful and energetic occasion. The event, often called the Ghost Festival, is distinguished by colorful processions in which participants don elaborate masks and costumes to become ghosts and spirits.

Although the festival originated as a part of a customary Buddhist ceremony meant to merit something, it has grown into a colorful and captivating event that attracts visitors from all over the world. Phi Ta Khon, with its unique costumes, music, and youthful attitude, is a cultural festival not to be missed.

Nightclubs and Entertainment Hotspots in Bangkok: Capital of the Urban Beat

Bangkok, the bustling metropolis at the center of Thailand, has a vibrant and diverse nightlife scene. For those looking to dance the night away or take in live entertainment, the city offers a plethora of options. These alternatives include vibrant entertainment districts and world-class nightclubs.

Along Sukhumvit Road, especially in the neighboring neighborhoods of Nana and Thonglor, there are a lot of pubs and nightclubs. Places like Levels Club, Insanity Nightclub, and Sing Sing Theater are some of the city's most well-liked nighttime attractions. These places are well-known for drawing lively patrons, themed parties, and well-known DJs.

Beach Parties in the Phi Phi Islands: A Tropical Carnival

The Phi Phi Islands, which are especially well-known for their gorgeous beaches and immaculate waters, have a vibrant nightlife scene. Beach parties at Tonsai Village, Koh Phi Phi Don, come alive as the sun sets and draw partygoers from all over the world. The lively atmosphere is enhanced by activities like fire displays, live music, and seaside bars, which allow visitors to take in the island's tropical splendor under the stars.

Thailand's festivals and nightlife offer a wide range of experiences, from the exciting customs of cultural celebrations to the pulsating beats of urban nightclubs. There are many different festivals and nightlife events in Bangkok. Every single encounter adds to the vibrant tapestry of Thai culture, be it releasing lanterns during Loy Krathong, enjoying the energy of a Full Moon Party, or fully immersing oneself in the joyous spirit of Songkran.

As you enjoy the vibrant evenings and festive treats that Thailand has to offer, you will learn that this is a nation that knows how to celebrate life with vigor and kindness. Thailand's festivals and nightlife entice visitors to join in the joyous celebrations that epitomize this captivating country in Southeast Asia. Anywhere from the busy streets of Bangkok to the serene beaches of Koh Phangan may host these events.

Chapter 8:
Souvenirs And Shopping In Thailand

Thailand, a nation renowned for its vibrant culture and diverse scenery, is also praised for the unique and unusual shopping experiences it provides. Thailand offers a wealth of opportunities for shopping and souvenir-seeking, ranging from upscale malls to vibrant street vendors and crowded marketplaces. In this chapter, we will explore the art of shopping in the Land of Smiles and discover the wide range of gifts that aptly encapsulate Thailand's essence.

Thai Traditional Crafts: Artisanal Beauty

Fine traditional goods that are a reflection of Thailand's rich cultural history are available for purchase when you go shopping there. One of the best things about shopping in Thailand is this. By searching the marketplaces and artist communities, travelers can find handcrafted items like intricate Thai silk, exquisite porcelain, and intricately carved wooden crafts.

In places like Chiang Mai, traditional crafts can find refuge at the Night Bazaar. It sells a broad range of goods, from ornately designed cutlery to silk scarves. These authentic pieces, which represent Thailand's cultural legacy in addition to being charming souvenirs, showcase the country's workmanship and artistic traditions.

Thai Silk: Grace in Each Weave

If you want to add a little elegance to your collection, Thai silk is a must-have memory. It is well known for its lustrous feel and shine throughout the entire world. Thailand's silk is distinguished by its rich designs and vibrant colors, which are a reflection of the nation's artistic past. Silk goods come in all shapes and sizes, and they can be used to make clothing, accessories, and even home décor pieces.

The renowned American businessman Jim Thompson, who played a significant role in bringing back the silk industry in Thailand, owns a renowned home and store in Bangkok. Thompson had a major role in the resurgence of the silk trade. For those looking to add a touch of classic elegance to their homes, there are several options available, and the Jim Thompson brand is well-known for producing superior Thai silk.

Elephant-Themed Memorabilia: A Sign of Thailand

In Thai culture, the elephant symbolizes strength, wisdom, and good fortune, giving it a special and important place. Travelers may find a huge selection of elephant-themed trinkets in Thailand. These include elephant-shaped sculptures, textiles with elephant patterns, and even painstakingly crafted wooden elephants.

In addition to viewing an array of artistically painted elephant sculptures, the Elephant Parade House in Chiang Mai offers a wide range of elephant-themed merchandise for sale. Buying these mementos not only allows you to have a unique keepsake but also helps support Thailand's efforts to conserve elephant populations.

Bangkok's Chatuchak Weekend Market is a shoppers' paradise

Visiting the Chatuchak Weekend Market in Bangkok is a must for every well-rounded shopping trip in Thailand. This massive market is a veritable gold mine, offering everything from home décor and antiques to apparel and accessories. It is a maze of gems with over 8,000 dealers spread across 27 areas.

Guests have the chance to take in the vibrant ambiance, barter prices with the friendly sellers, and find unique finds everywhere they look. Chatuchak is more than just a market; it's an amazing experience that captures the variety of shopping options available in Thailand.

Talismans & Amulets: Spiritual Treasures

Talismans and amulets are well-established symbols in Thai culture. They are believed to bestow upon the wearer protection, prosperity, and spiritual blessings. There is a wide variety of amulets available for purchase by tourists, from simple amulets from street vendors to exquisitely crafted and auspiciously blessed amulets from well-known temples.

Wat Phra Kaew, a popular tourist destination in Bangkok, is well-known for its sacred amulets. Purchasing and donning these amulets is an important way to connect with Thailand's spiritual traditions in addition to serving as a keepsake of your trip.

Floating Markets: Gastronomic and Cultural Treats

Thailand's floating markets provide more than just shopping opportunities—they are fully immersive cultural experiences. The Damnoen Saduak Floating Market, which is near Bangkok, is one of the most well-known floating markets. Here, many vendors operate boats along the canals, peddling their wares.

Along with enjoying the colorful and appealing surroundings, visitors may browse for locally made products like fresh produce, snacks, and handcrafted items. Experience the Floating Market, a unique blend of contemporary business and traditional Thai culture, for an unmatched flavor of Thailand's vibrant market scene.

Jewelry & Gemstones: Thai Artistry

Thailand is renowned for its exceptional gemstone industry and offers an extensive range of precious and semi-precious stones. By perusing the numerous jewelry stores and markets, tourists can acquire beautifully crafted pieces that showcase gemstones from Thailand, including jade, rubies, and sapphires.

The Gem and Jewelry District in Bangkok is a popular destination for those who enjoy gem buying. Whether a customer is searching for a delicate piece of jewelry or loose gemstones to utilize in the production of unique creations, the gemstone market in Thailand offers a wide range of options to suit their interests and tastes.

Contemporary Malls: Retail Rehab in Metropolitan Areas

Instead of visiting Thailand's traditional marketplaces, visitors seeking upscale clothing, international brands, and a modern shopping experience will find what they're searching for in the country's modern shopping malls. Bangkok is home to some of the world's most renowned retail complexes, including CentralWorld, EmQuartier, and Siam Paragon.

These shopping centers provide both domestic and foreign brands in addition to a range of entertainment venues, fine dining establishments, and even indoor ice skating rinks. The modern malls in Thailand offer a fresh shopping experience that may be enjoyable for those who value having a lot of selections and air-conditioned areas.

You may view shopping in Thailand as an art form that blends traditional craftsmanship, cultural treasures, and modern retail experiences. Every shopping excursion in Thailand offers a different perspective on the diverse landscape of the nation, whether you're navigating the congested aisles of Chatuchak Market, appreciating the timeless elegance of Thai silk, or accepting the spiritual meaning of amulets.

As you start your shopping adventure in the Land of Smiles, remember that every memento holds a little piece of Thailand's rich history and culture in addition to your memories of the trip. Thailand invites you to experience the thrill of exploration and to bring home mementos that embodie this amazing country in Southeast Asia. Everything you could possibly want may be found in Thailand, from the elegant malls to the quaint street markets.

Chapter 9:
Photography and Social Media:

Social media and photography are now closely related in the context of the current digital era. Due to the widespread use of smartphones with high-end cameras and the widespread appeal of social networking sites like Facebook, Instagram, and Twitter, sharing photographs has become a vital part of our daily lives. Even though recording and sharing events can be enjoyable, it is important to respect other people's privacy as well as the environment when doing so. This essay will cover the concept of photo-worthy locations and offer some practical advice for responsibly sharing photos on social media.

Photo-worthy Locations:

One of the most exciting things about photography is the process of finding and photographing places that are worth photographing. These can include both well-known sites and hidden gems that are off the typical route. The following things should be kept in mind when locating and taking pictures of these areas:

1. Research and Exploration: It's crucial to get ready by doing a thorough investigation into appropriate locations before starting a photography adventure. Finding unique places can be achieved by browsing through travel blogs, neighborhood guides, and photo forums. Sometimes the most breathtaking places are just in your own backyard, so be open to exploring your surroundings and keep an open mind.
2. Iconic Landmarks: Iconic locations are commonly used in photography, and this is a totally understandable decision. They add an invaluable sense of beauty, culture, and

history. When you are photographing these kinds of places, try to capture them from unique angles or at different times of the day to offer a different perspective.
3. Natural Beauty: There are countless photogenic locations in nature to choose from. The magnificent beauty of the natural world, which includes everything from majestic mountains and serene lakes to lush woods and breathtaking beaches, is something that can never be sufficiently appreciated. It is crucial to practice environmental awareness and follow the Leave No Trace guidelines in order to protect these places' natural beauty for future generations.
4. Urban Exploration: Cities offer a plethora of intriguing and distinctive locations for photographers to work with. Street art, architectural wonders, and urban panoramas are a few examples of things that might be appealing. You can experiment with capturing the life and essence of a city by exploring its many neighborhoods.

Cultural Riches: The cultural features of a location are the key to capturing the essence of that location. Local markets, festivals, or even just ordinary life could fall under this category. It is important to interact with the community in a polite manner, to ask for permission when it is required, and to portray their tales in an honest manner.

How to Share Content on Social Media in a Responsible Manner:

It is essential to act properly when publishing your photographs on social media, despite the fact that doing so can be a richly satisfying experience. Here are some suggestions to help you make sure that your presence on the internet makes a beneficial contribution to the community of digital users:

1. Respect for Privacy: When taking pictures of someone, you should always put their right to privacy and consent first.

Obtaining consent from the individuals whose faces appear in your photo is crucial if you want to share it on social media. When taking pictures of intimate or private situations, you should exercise discretion and refrain from uploading any images that might infringe on someone else's personal space.
2. Conscientious Tagging: It's critical to consider the location when uploading photos to social media and tag them appropriately. When in doubt, keep quiet about promoting private or isolated locations that might suffer from an influx of more tourists. The authenticity of photogenic places is preserved in part by a conscientious tagging system.
3. Give the background: Tell the tale that your pictures are hiding beneath. This can include the background of a well-known landmark, your own experiences, or the location's cultural significance. Including context not only makes your articles more insightful for readers, but it also provides them additional depth.
4. Employ Captions Carefully: Write descriptions that will help the audience understand the picture more fully and value it more. Use your captions to express emotions, share interesting information, or invite comments from your audience. A well-written caption may take an ordinary snapshot and turn it into a deep narrative experience.
5. Be Aware of Image Editing: Although image editing software can enhance the visual attractiveness of your photos, you should use it with caution. Extensive modification is not something you should do if you want to avoid misrepresenting the reality of a location. Authenticity is a crucial element in building trust with your audience.
6. Engage Positively: By communicating politely with your audience, you may create a community that is positive and supportive. Make the effort to reply to remarks, encourage

beneficial dialogue, and remain receptive to criticism. Utilize your position to inspire and uplift those around you.
7. Encourage Environmental Responsibility: If the landscape in your photos is natural, you should inspire others to take environmental responsibility seriously. Encourage those who are listening to you to take up eco-friendly habits, be mindful of wildlife, and lessen their environmental impact. Make the most of your considerable influence to promote environmental conservation.
8. Recognize the Platform Policies: Regarding the publishing of content, each social media platform has its own rules and regulations. To avoid inadvertent violations, it is crucial that you familiarize yourself with these rules. Crediting others when appropriate and adhering to copyright regulations are both important.
9. Social media and photography are a powerful combo that you may use to share moments, experiences, and stories with people worldwide. If we engage in responsible site discovery and post photos of worthy sites, we can potentially contribute positively to the online community. Every picture has a narrative to tell, and it is our duty to ensure that that story is communicated with dignity, sincerity, and regard for other people. Remember that every picture tells a narrative, whether we are documenting the majesty of nature, the energy of city life, or the diversity of civilizations.

Chapter 10:
Tips For Traveling in Thailand

Thailand's diverse landscape, rich cultural heritage, and friendly populace make it an enthralling travel destination. It is essential that you arm yourself with useful tips as you get ready to embark on your journey through the Land of Smiles to ensure a convenient and unforgettable travel experience. We will provide you with a thorough guidance in this chapter to help you make the most of your trip and navigate Thailand with confidence.

1. **Respect Local Customs and Etiquette: The Heart of Thai Culture**

Thailand has deeply rooted traditional values and a good sense of social responsibility. Understanding and following the norms and etiquette of the place is crucial. It is crucial to remember that:

a. Wai Greeting: The wai is a traditional Thai greeting that involves kneeling slightly and putting your palms together in a way akin to a prayer. This is an obvious act of respect, and it should be given back.

a. Modest Clothing: When visiting temples and places of worship, it is appropriate to dress modestly, which includes covering your shoulders and knees. This guideline does not apply to men or women in particular.

c. Shoes Off Indoors: It is customary to remove your shoes before entering any type of temple, certain businesses, and homes. Look for signs or do what the locals do and follow their lead.

d. Respect for the Monarchy: The Thai people hold their monarchy in the highest regard. Critiquing or disregarding the royal family is considered offensive, and depending on the situation, it may lead to legal repercussions.

2. **Learn Basic Thai Phrases: Bridge the Language Barrier**

Even if English is widely spoken in tourist areas, it remains advantageous to attempt to learn a few basic Thai words so that you may converse with locals:

A salutation of "Sawasdee" b. gratitude "Mai Chai" d. No: "Khob Khun" e. Yes: "Chai" c. I apologize. Excuse me, Khor thoad.

It's appreciated by Thai people when guests try to communicate in their language, so you'll probably be greeted with smiles and kindness.

3. **Be Mindful of the Weather: Thailand's Seasons and Climates**

In Thailand, there are three distinct seasons to be aware of: the hot season, which runs from March to June, the rainy season, and the cold, dry season, which runs from November to February (July to October). It is crucial that you pack according to the plans you have for your trip. You should be ready for both the likelihood of rain and extremely high humidity during the rainy season.

Temperatures may be cooler while visiting northern or mountainous areas, especially in the evenings. This is particularly valid if you're traveling to a mountainous region. It's critical to keep yourself informed about the weather in any location you plan to visit in order to guarantee a relaxing and enjoyable vacation.

4. **Health and Safety: Prioritize Your Well-being**

Keep Hydrated: It's important to drink lots of water because Thailand's weather may be hot and muggy. Avoid using tap water and instead sip on plenty of water from bottles.

a. Health Precautions: Before visiting Thailand, find out from your doctor what vaccinations are advised. Wear long sleeves in the evenings and use bug repellent because dengue and other mosquito-borne illnesses are common.

c. Travel Insurance: You should consider getting comprehensive travel insurance that covers medical emergencies, trip cancellations, and personal belongings damage. As a result, in the unlikely case of an unforeseen circumstance, one can have financial security and peace of mind.

d. Traffic and Transportation Safety: It's crucial to exercise caution when crossing streets, particularly in crowded urban areas. It is crucial to use designated crosswalks whenever possible and to be aware of any local traffic restrictions. When using public transportation, pick options with a solid reputation and make sure to use the seat belts, if provided.

5. **Transportation Tips: Navigating Thailand's Diverse Landscape**

a. Taxis and Tuk-Tuks: Taxis should always use meters, and it's wise to haggle over the fare while taking a tuk-tuk. Extremely demanding drivers ought to be avoided; instead, go with qualified services.

a. Public Transportation: Thailand's vast and well-connected networks include buses, trains, and boats. Both the Bangkok Skytrain (BTS) and the MRT subway system are efficient ways to move about the nation's capital.

c. Renting Motorcycles: Make sure you are wearing a helmet and that you have the appropriate license when you rent a motorcycle. Acquaint oneself with the traffic laws and road conditions in your area.

d. Domestic Flights: Consider taking long-distance flights within Thailand on domestic airlines. It is an efficient way to travel large distances in a short amount of time, and many airlines provide affordable options.

6. **Currency and Money Matters: Practical Financial Tips**

a. Thai Baht: The Thai Baht is the official currency of the Thai government (THB). Acquaint yourself with the current exchange rates and take advantage of reputable currency exchange companies.

a. ATMs: You can find automated teller machines (ATMs) all over major cities and popular tourist destinations. To prevent any issues when using your credit or debit card while you are away, you should notify your bank of the dates of your vacation.

c. Cash vs. Credit Cards: Although large credit cards are accepted in urban areas, cash is preferred in smaller towns and local marketplaces. Having both cash and cards on you is more practical.

d. Bargaining: When it comes to street vendors and souvenirs, bargaining is a regular occurrence in marketplaces. Be ready to bargain and take a pleasant stance when approaching it.

7. **Explore Beyond Tourist Hotspots: Hidden Gems Await**

Even while visiting well-known locations like Bangkok, Phuket, and Chiang Mai is vital, you should also consider visiting lesser-known locations in Thailand to fully appreciate the actual charm of the nation:

a. Island Hopping: Exploring destinations outside of the well-known islands. There are less people on Koh Lanta, Koh Tao, and Koh Chang, all of which provide unique experiences.

a. Northern Treasures: The rich cultural heritage of northern Thailand can be found in locations like Pai, Mae Hong Son, and Nan, which are distinguished by their picturesque landscapes and charming communities.

c. Isan Region: For a flavor of the native way of life, a wealth of historical sites, and historic temples, explore the northeastern part of Isan.

d. Local Markets: Get a taste of real Thai food and see daily life by visiting local markets that are not close to tourist attractions.

8. **Embrace the Culinary Adventure: Thai Food Delights**

Thai food is well known throughout the world for its varied dishes and strong flavors. Take on the gastronomic journey with these suggestions:

a. Street Food Exploration: Thai street food is a delicious gastronomic experience. Visit the neighborhood markets and street vendors to sample authentic dishes like Pad Thai, Mango Sticky Rice, and Som Tum (green papaya salad).

b. Hygiene Safety Measures: Even though street food is usually safe, choose vendors with tidy and active stalls to avoid any problems. Make sure the food is cooked all the way through.

c. Spicy: Thai food has a tendency to be spicy. Inform the chef of your preference if you're not used to a lot of spice so they can adjust the amount.

d. Dining Etiquette: It is usual to hold off on starting to eat until the host or the oldest person has done so. Thai people like eating together by sharing meals in a family-style manner.

9. Cultural Sensitivity: Appreciating Local Traditions

a. Temples & Religious Sites: You should wear modestly, covering your knees and shoulders, when visiting temples. You are required to take off your shoes before you enter the temple's structures.

b. Foot Etiquette: It's customary to refrain from pointing your feet toward people or sacred objects because it's thought that the feet are the lowest part of the body.

c. Cultural Events and Festivals: It's crucial to respect the traditions being upheld and to participate with a genuine desire to learn about the regional customs whenever you attend cultural events or festivals.

d. Respect for the Environment: Preventing actions that harm coral reefs, marine life, or natural habitats is a critical first step in environmental protection. Travel with consideration for the environment and dispose of trash properly.

10. Connect with Locals: Enrich Your Journey

The relationships formed with locals are the essence of any trip experience. The following advice can help to promote deep conversations:

a. Acquaint Yourself with Local Customs: Give local greetings, customs, and social conventions some thought. Respect for the culture is highly valued by the locals.

a. Participate in Local Events: Attending festivals, ceremonies, or other events in the community gives you a better understanding of its customs and gives you a chance to meet locals.

c. Homestays and Community Tourism: To experience daily living and boost local economies, think about participating in community-based tourism or staying in homestays.

d. Language Exchange: Speaking with locals in their native tongue might help you gain a better understanding of Thai culture. Many Thai people are willing to converse in English and impart their national expertise.

Thailand's interesting blend of traditional and modern aspects encourages visitors to explore the country's diverse landscapes and immerse themselves in its rich culture. Thanks to the incredibly useful advice you have been given, you are now well-equipped to navigate the Kingdom and make the most of your tour through the Land of Smiles.

Thailand offers a diverse range of events that will linger long in your memory. Thailand offers a plethora of experiences, including wandering through bustling marketplaces, savoring delicious street cuisine, and exploring historic temples. As you set off on an incredible voyage through the world of travel, embrace the excitement, interact with the locals, and let Thailand's character blossom before you.

Chapter 11:
Frequent Asked Questions About Thailand

1. **here is Thailand located?**
   - Thailand is a country in Southeast Asia, bordered by Myanmar to the northwest, Laos to the northeast, Cambodia to the southeast, and Malaysia to the south.
2. **What is the capital of Thailand?**
   - Bangkok.
3. **What is the official language of Thailand?**
   - Thai.
4. **What is the currency in Thailand?**
   - Thai Baht (THB).
5. **What is the time zone in Thailand?**
   - Indochina Time (ICT), UTC+7.
6. **Is Thailand safe for tourists?**
   - Generally, Thailand is considered safe for tourists. However, like any destination, it's essential to exercise common-sense precautions.
7. **Do I need a visa to visit Thailand?**
   - It depends on your nationality and the purpose of your visit. Check the visa requirements before traveling.
8. **What is the best time to visit Thailand?**
   - November to February is the cool and dry season, making it the most popular time to visit.
9. **What is the national symbol of Thailand?**
   - The Garuda, a mythical bird creature.

Culture and Etiquette:

10. **What is the traditional greeting in Thailand?**
    - The traditional greeting is the wai, a gesture of

pressing the palms together in a prayer-like manner.
11. **Is it appropriate to tip in Thailand?**
    - Tipping is not mandatory, but it is appreciated. A 10% service charge is often included in restaurants.
12. **What is considered polite behavior in Thailand?**
    - Showing respect for elders, avoiding public displays of anger, and removing shoes before entering someone's home are considered polite.
13. **Can I wear shorts in temples?**
    - While shorts are generally acceptable in Thailand, they are not appropriate for temple visits. Wear long pants or a long skirt when entering temples.

Food and Drink:

14. **What is the staple food in Thailand?**
    - Rice is a staple, and Thai cuisine is known for its use of aromatic herbs and spices.
15. **Is Thai food always spicy?**
    - Thai food can be spicy, but not all dishes are. You can specify your spice level when ordering.
16. **What is the traditional Thai meal structure?**
    - A typical meal includes rice, a meat or fish dish, a soup, and vegetables.
17. **Is it safe to drink tap water in Thailand?**
    - It's advisable to drink bottled or boiled water. Tap water may not be safe for consumption.

Transportation:

18. **How is the public transportation system in Thailand?**
    - Thailand has a well-developed transportation system, including buses, trains, and tuk-tuks. Bangkok also has an extensive BTS Skytrain and MRT subway system.
19. **Do I need an international driver's license to rent a car?**
    - Yes, it is recommended to have an international

driver's license to rent a car.
20. **Are tuk-tuks safe?**
    - Tuk-tuks are a common mode of transportation, but negotiate the fare before the ride and be cautious about scams.

Health and Safety:

21. **Are vaccinations required for traveling to Thailand?**
    - Some vaccinations are recommended, like hepatitis A and B, typhoid, and Japanese encephalitis. Check with a healthcare professional before traveling.
22. **What is the healthcare system like in Thailand?**
    - Thailand has both public and private healthcare facilities. Private hospitals in major cities offer high-quality care.
23. **Is there a risk of malaria in Thailand?**
    - Malaria is present in certain areas, especially rural regions. Consult a healthcare professional for advice on malaria prevention.

Shopping:

24. **Is bargaining common in Thailand?**
    - Bargaining is common in markets and smaller shops, but not in department stores or malls.
25. **What are popular souvenirs to buy in Thailand?**
    - Thai silk, handicrafts, traditional clothing, and spices are popular souvenirs.

Tourist Attractions:

26. **What are the must-visit places in Bangkok?**
    - Grand Palace, Wat Pho, Wat Arun, and Chatuchak Weekend Market are popular attractions.
27. **Are there beautiful beaches in Thailand?**

- Yes, Thailand is famous for its stunning beaches, including those in Phuket, Krabi, and Koh Samui.
28. **Can I visit the Phi Phi Islands on a day trip?**
    - Yes, day trips to the Phi Phi Islands are common, but staying overnight is recommended to fully enjoy the beauty.

Accommodation:

29. **What types of accommodation are available in Thailand?**
    - Thailand offers a range of accommodations, from budget hostels to luxury resorts. Guesthouses and boutique hotels are also popular.
30. **Is it necessary to book accommodation in advance?**
    - It's advisable, especially during peak tourist seasons.

Technology and Communication:

31. **Is there widespread internet access in Thailand?**
    - Yes, there is widespread internet access, and most hotels, restaurants, and cafes offer free Wi-Fi.
32. **Can I use my mobile phone in Thailand?**
    - Yes, most international mobile phones work in Thailand. You can also easily get a local SIM card.

Currency and Banking:

33. **Can I use credit cards in Thailand?**
    - Credit cards are widely accepted in urban areas, but cash is preferred in more rural locations.
34. **Are there ATMs in Thailand?**
    - Yes, ATMs are common in urban areas. Inform your bank about your travel plans to avoid card issues.

Nightlife:

35. **What is the nightlife like in Thailand?**
    - Thailand is known for its vibrant nightlife, especially in cities like Bangkok and Pattaya.
36. **Are there any specific dress codes for nightlife?**
    - Dress codes can vary, but many venues may have a smart casual dress code.

Festivals:

37. **What are the major festivals in Thailand?**
    - Songkran (Thai New Year), Loy Krathong, and Yi Peng Lantern Festival are major celebrations.
38. **How is Songkran celebrated?**
    - Songkran is celebrated with water fights, symbolizing cleansing and renewal.

Language:

39. **Do people in Thailand speak English?**
    - In tourist areas and major cities, many people speak English. Learning a few basic Thai phrases is appreciated.

Wildlife:

40. **Can I ride elephants in Thailand?**
    - It's discouraged to ride elephants due to concerns about animal welfare. Consider visiting ethical elephant sanctuaries instead.
41. **Are there dangerous animals in Thailand?**
    - While encounters are rare, Thailand is home to some venomous snakes and insects. Be cautious in rural areas.

Religion:

42. **What is the predominant religion in Thailand?**
    - Buddhism is the predominant religion, and you'll find many temples across the country.
43. **Are there any etiquette rules when visiting temples?**
    - Dress modestly, remove shoes before entering, and avoid pointing your feet at Buddha statues.

Customs and Laws:

44. **Is it illegal to disrespect the king in Thailand?**
    - Yes, Thailand has strict lèse-majesté laws, and disrespecting the king can lead to severe consequences.
45. **What is the legal drinking age in Thailand?**
    - The legal drinking age is 20.

Weather:

46. **Does Thailand experience monsoons?**
    - Yes, Thailand has a monsoon season, usually from June to October.
47. **Is it safe to visit during the monsoon season?**
    - While travel is still possible, some areas may experience flooding. Check weather forecasts and plan accordingly.

Local Transportation:

48. **What is the most common mode of local transportation?**
    - Taxis, tuk-tuks, and motorbike taxis are common for short-distance travel.
49. **Is it safe to use motorbike taxis?**
    - Use reputable services, wear a helmet, and negotiate the fare before the ride.
50. **How is traffic in Bangkok?**
    - Traffic in Bangkok can be congested, especially during rush hours. The BTS Skytrain and MRT subway are

recommended for avoiding traffic.

Conclusion

We are not just at the conclusion of a book. Instead, it marks the beginning of a new chapter in the journey story you have been collecting. It is not just the conclusion of a book that we are celebrating as we draw the final curtain on this journey across the mesmerizing landscapes and diverse cultures of Thailand. Thailand is a country that is well-renowned for its diverse cultures and breathtaking beauty, and this trip has taken you across the entirety of a country that is known for both of these things. Together, we have set out on an adventure that will take us deep into the heart of the Land of Smiles, where we will uncover its mysteries and find the pearls that make Thailand a destination that cannot be compared to any other. Over the course of the subsequent few pages, this journey has been taking place that you are currently reading.

From the very beginning of its existence, this travel guide has been more than just a collection of useful ideas and locations that absolutely no one should miss out on seeing. It has been more than that. It has been a companion to you in the sense that it has been a travel companion, a confidant, and a curator of experiences that are individualized to your desire to travel. All of these things have been happening at the same time till now. You would not only be extended an invitation to travel to Thailand, but you would also be extended an opportunity to become a part of the narrative of the country. One would have the chance to experience the heartbeat of a nation that is abundant in history, culture, and the generosity of its people if they were to have this opportunity. In the event that we were able to condense the essence of this tour into a single remark, we would like to extend an invitation to visit to Thailand.

We have committed ourselves to achieving your travel objectives by providing you with experiences that are founded on the truth and that you will never forget. When we first started our investigation, we made this commitment to ourselves. Through the efforts that we have put out, we have been able to produce a discovery tapestry that appears as follows. A voyage into the very heart and soul of Thailand was whispered to the reader, and not only were they travel advice, but they were also a journey into the very heart and soul of Thailand. More than just travel advice, these pages included personal experiences, thoughts, and suggestions that may be found within them. You can find all of these things inside these pages. When we embarked on this journey, we did so with the understanding that traveling is not simply about visiting a series of locations; rather, it is about embracing the spirit of a location, becoming fully immersed in its culture, and making memories that will remain with us for a very long time after we have finished our journey and returned home.

As we have been studying the numerous issues that have been explored, which span from the bustling marketplaces of Bangkok to the calm getaways that are nestled away in the hills of the north, we have come across the cultural kaleidoscope that is the defining attribute of Thailand. During the course of our trip, we visited a variety of different places, some of which included the breathtaking beaches of the islands, where the sunsets are nothing short of amazing, and the historic splendors of Ayutthaya, where history can be heard echoing in the monuments. Both of these places were among the places that we visited. We came to the idea that Thai food is not only about taste, but rather a symphony of flavors that mirror the stories of generations that have come before us. This was a revelation to us. During the course of our exploration of the gastronomic marvels that Thailand has to offer, we came to this realization.

The purpose of this book was not merely to give you with a list of destinations to see; rather, it sought to arm you with the exact information and self-assurance you need in order to build your very own one-of-a-kind and unique experience while you are in Thailand. Taking advantage of the resources that are currently at your disposal, you will be able to take full advantage of the grandeur that Thailand has to offer at this particular moment in time. These characteristics include the capacity to acquire a comprehension of the cultural nuances as well as the capability to traverse the congested streets in a method that is efficient.

Additionally, in order to satisfy this pledge, it was necessary to take out additional procedures in addition to the fact that information was given. This was a vital step. It was vital to stimulate a passion for exploration that goes beyond the charms that are quickly obvious on the surface in order to develop a connection between you and the location. This enthusiasm should go beyond the charms that are readily apparent on the surface. Our goal was to be more than just a guide; we wanted to be a catalyst for experiences that are transformative. We aspired to be that which is greater than this. From the beginning, this was the plan. In order for you to be able to take advantage of the treasures that travel has to offer, we wanted to motivate you to try new things and push yourself beyond the boundaries of your comfort zone.

What is the one thing that I genuinely hope you will bear in mind when you reach the end of this paragraph, taking into consideration everything that has been said thus far? The notion that travel, at its core, is an expression of curiosity and a celebration of diversity is the foundation upon which this knowledge is built. This insight serves as the foundation upon which these statistics are built. Every single interaction that you have had, whether it be with locals in a bustling market or the tranquil setting of a hidden gem, has given you the opportunity to appreciate the fascinating differences that exist between individuals. Each and every one of these interactions has provided you with the opportunity to be a better person. It is possible for you to do so at this time. Every single one of them has made it possible for you to take advantage of this wonderful opportunity. To put it more accurately, Thailand is a tapestry that is woven with the threads of history, culture, and the expressions of the people who live there. This is a more true description of the country. The country of Thailand is more than just a vacation spot. When presented with the chance to visit to Thailand, one should not pass it up. I sincerely hope that you will carry with you on every journey that lies ahead of you a reverence for the vast number of people and cultures that exist, a desire to learn about new things, and the warmth of the welcome that you experienced in Thailand. I hope that you will take all of these things with you. I really hope that you bring these things with you wherever you go.

In spite of the fact that we are going to be separated for a period of time in the future, it is essential to keep in mind that the journey does not truly come to an end with the finish of this book. As a consequence of the experiences that you have had, Thailand will continue to evolve throughout the course of the years, and the story surrounding the nation will be enlarged to include additional layers. Continuing to make progress is something that is anticipated to occur in Thailand. Consequently, as you move beyond these pages and into the world beyond, bring with you the spirit of a traveler – one who is inquisitive, open-minded, and eager to explore the wonders that lie ahead.

This trip guide has been written with the intention of releasing the adventurer that is already present within you, rather than solely concentrating on Thailand as its primary destination. This has been the organization's principal goal throughout its existence. I wish that the reverberations of the Land of Smiles will follow you wherever you go, providing as a continual reminder that every single area is a blank canvas simply waiting to be painted with your own personal approach to doing things. I hope that this will happen. It is important that reverberations such as these serve as a constant reminder. I hope that your adventures are just as adventurous and exciting as the stories that are woven across these pages. I am an adventurer myself. I wish you a safe voyage and I hope that the experiences you have along the way will be unforgettable. While you are embarking on this journey, know that you are in my thoughts and prayers.

Printed in Great Britain
by Amazon